★ IT'S MY STATE! ★

CONNECTICUT

Michael Burgan

Stephanie Fitzgerald

Marshall Cavendish
Benchmark

New York

Other Marshall Cavendish Offices:
Marshall Cavendish International (Asia) Private Limited, 1 New Industrial Road, Singapore 536196 •
Marshall Cavendish International (Thailand) Co Ltd. 253 Asoke, 12th Flr, Sukhumvit 21 Road, Klongtoey Nua, Wattana, Bangkok 10110, Thailand • Marshall Cavendish (Malaysia) Sdn Bhd, Times Subang, Lot 46, Subang Hi-Tech Industrial Park, Batu Tiga, 40000 Shah Alam, Selangor Darul Ehsan, Malaysia

Marshall Cavendish is a trademark of Times Publishing Limited

All websites were available and accurate when this book was sent to press.

Library of Congress Cataloging-in-Publication Data
Burgan, Michael.
          Connecticut / Michael Burgan, Stephanie Fitzgerald. — 2nd ed.
              p. cm. — (It's my state!)
          Includes index.
          ISBN 978-1-60870-047-9
          1. Connecticut—Juvenile literature. I. Fitzgerald, Stephanie. II. Title.
          F94.3.B87 2011
          974.6—dc22   2010003917

Second Edition developed for Marshall Cavendish Benchmark by RJF Publishing LLC (www.RJFpublishing.com)
Series Designer, Second Edition: Tammy West/Westgraphix LLC
Editor, Second Edition: Emily Dolbear

All maps, illustrations, and graphics © Marshall Cavendish Corporation. Maps and artwork on pages 6, 30, 31, and back cover by Christopher Santoro. Map and graphics on pages 8 and 41 by Westgraphix LLC. Map on page 76 by Mapping Specialists.

The photographs in this book are used by permission and through the courtesy of:
Front cover: Fraser Hall and Jim Jordan Photography (inset)/Getty Images.
Alamy: Peter Arnold, Inc, 10; Danita Delimont, 11, 74; Jon Arnold Images Ltd., 12; Corbis AGStockUSA, 13; fStop, 38; Nancy Catherine Walker, 42; Peter Glass, 46; Enigma, 48, 53; Kokyat Choong, 50; Michael Doolittle, 51; Franck Fotos, 52; Andre Jenny, 62. **AP Images:** Bob Child, 57.
Corbis: 20; © Franz-Marc Frei, 43. **Getty Images:** Darlyne A. Murawski/National Geographic, 4; Manfred Pfefferle (top) and Hulton Archive (bottom), 5; Mitchell Funk, 9; Kindra Clineff, 14; Tier Und Naturfotografie J & C Sohns (top) and DAJ (bottom), 15; Tyler Stableford, 16; Joseph Van Os, 17; De Agostini, 18; Joe McDonald (top), 19; Hulton Archive, 22, 24, 26; Stock Montage/Hulton Archives, 29, 44; MPI/Hulton Archives, 32-3; Time & Life Pictures, 34; Bob Falcetti, 40; Imagno/Hulton Archvies, 45; Murat Taner, 54; Steve Dunwell, 68-9; Gary Buss, 73. **Lee Snider:** 59.
Shutterstock: SchneiderStockImages (bottom), 19; FloridaStock, 28; Michael Mattox, 49; Sharon Kennedy, 61; RixPix, 64; teekaygee, 65; Steve Mann, 66; Ritu Manoj Jethani , 70; Sereda Nikolay Ivanovich, 72 (top); eGraphia, 72 (bottom).

Printed in Malaysia (T).
135642

CONNECTICUT

CONTENTS

A Quick Look at
CONNECTICUT

State Flower: Mountain Laurel

Connecticut's state flower is the mountain laurel. This shrub has poisonous leaves, but it also has beautiful white-and-pink flowers that bloom from May to July. Mountain laurels thrive in the woodlands of Connecticut and can grow as high as 15 feet (4.6 meters).

State Bird: American Robin

Early settlers called this songbird a robin because it looked like the robins found in Europe. But the American robin is actually a thrush—the largest in North America. The American robin is a sure sign of spring in Connecticut. But some of these birds also spend the winter in the state, eating the berries that grow on evergreen trees.

State Tree: Charter Oak (White Oak)

Connecticut's state tree is a white oak named the Charter Oak, which once grew in Hartford. According to legend, the Charter Oak was once used to hide Connecticut's charter, a political document that ensured the state's rights as an English colony. In 1687, the colonists hid the charter to save their government. Unfortunately, the Charter Oak fell during a storm in 1856.

State Insect: European Mantis

Connecticut's state insect is also called a praying mantis, because its two front legs are close together, like hands during prayer. It lives in the state from May or June until the cold weather starts. The praying mantis eats flies and other insects. Farmers find that mantises help control crop-eating caterpillars and aphids.

State Fossil: *Eubrontes giganteus*

More than 200 million years ago, a meat-eating dinosaur roamed the land that is now the Connecticut River Valley. The fossilized three-toed footprints that this dinosaur left are called *Eubrontes giganteus*. About two thousand of these stony prints are located at Dinosaur State Park in Rocky Hill. Unfortunately, no one has found any skeletal remains of the dinosaurs that made these tracks.

State Ship: The *Nautilus*

At the Submarine Force Library and Museum in Groton, Connecticut honors its strong ties to the sea with the USS *Nautilus*. This submarine, built in Groton, operated for twenty-five years. The *Nautilus* was the world's first ship to run on nuclear power, which allowed it to stay underwater for several weeks at a time. Connecticut's state ship is a National Historic Landmark.

The Constitution State

Connecticut is a small state with a long name. It is one of the six New England states that form the northeastern corner of the United States. The other five New England states are Maine, New Hampshire, Vermont, Massachusetts, and Rhode Island. Connecticut is almost rectangular, and it has what looks like a handle sticking out of the southwestern corner. The state, which contains eight counties, is 110 miles (177 kilometers) wide from east to west. Its north-south length is 70 miles (113 km). Connecticut's land area covers 4,845 square miles (12,548 sq km). Only the states of Delaware and Rhode Island are smaller.

The surface of Connecticut was formed over millions of years. Giant slabs of rock called tectonic plates lie deep beneath the earth's surface. Over time these plates have shifted, moving the land above. Continents and oceans were formed through this shifting. The plates' movement also helped to create the landscape on the earth's surface. Then, about 18,000 years ago, sheets of ice covered what is now Connecticut and other parts of North America. Among the sheets were large masses of ice called glaciers. As the

> ### Quick Facts
> **CONNECTICUT BORDERS**
>
> | | |
> |---|---|
> | **North** | Massachusetts |
> | **South** | New York (Long Island Sound) |
> | **East** | Rhode Island |
> | **West** | New York |

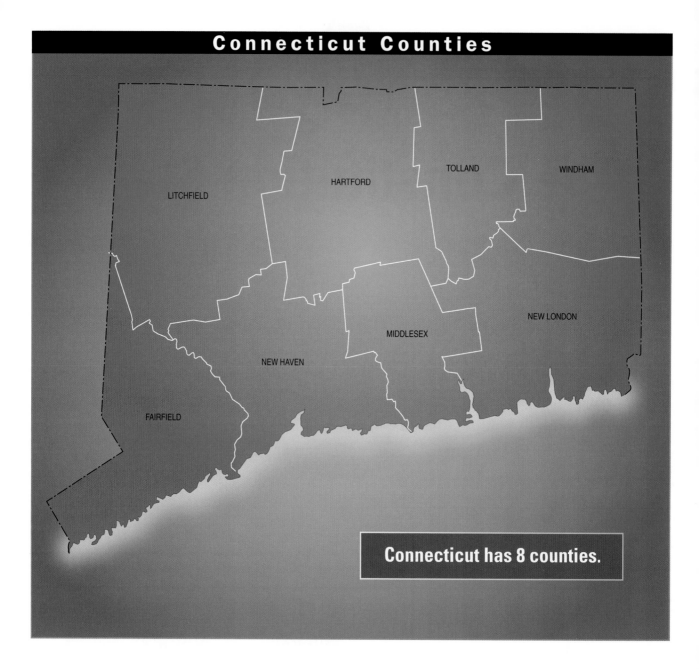

Connecticut has 8 counties.

glaciers moved, they carved out valleys. When the ice began to melt, soil and rocks were deposited across the land, helping to shape hills and other rocky features.

In general, the eastern and western portions of Connecticut are very rocky and not good for farming. But the central portion of the state is a fertile valley. The state can be divided into four major regions: the Connecticut River Valley, the Coastal Lowlands, the Western Uplands, and the Eastern Uplands.

River and Coast

The Connecticut River dominates the center of the state. At 410 miles (660 km) long, it is the longest river in New England. The river starts in a lake sitting between New Hampshire and Canada. Moving south, it forms the border between New Hampshire and Vermont, and it then passes through Massachusetts and Connecticut. The Connecticut River's course is fairly straight in the northern half of the state. Then it twists and turns a few times as it runs down to Long Island Sound. Shallow waters and sandbars—ridges of sand formed by waves and currents—make it hard to sail at the mouth of the river. Unlike many large U.S. rivers, the Connecticut does not have a major port or city at its mouth. Still, the river has been an important waterway for moving goods and people.

Fishing on the Connecticut River is a favorite pastime for many Nutmeggers.

By the 1960s, pollution choked the waters of the Connecticut River. The factories and towns along the river had been dumping waste into it for more than one hundred years. The New England states and the U.S. government have spent millions of dollars to clean up the river. Today, parts of the river are clean enough for swimming, and professional fishers come to Hartford for an annual fishing contest.

The land on either side of the river is called the Connecticut Valley or Central Valley. The water from the river makes the valley perfect for growing crops. The various American Indians of Connecticut were the first to farm this land. The rich

The Connecticut River Valley's fertile soil is ideal for farming.

farmland also drew Europeans to the area. Connecticut's capital, Hartford, sits on the western bank of the river. After riding through the Connecticut River Valley near Hartford in 1771, future president John Adams wrote, "I have spent this morning . . . riding through paradise; my eyes never beheld so fine a country."

At the south end of the river is Long Island Sound. The land that stretches along the length of the sound forms another region of Connecticut. It is sometimes called the Coastal Lowlands or Coastal Slope. The land here is mostly flat. Small coves cut into the shoreline, which also has marshlands. Long Island Sound has been polluted in the past. Some of the pollution came from the waste of cities along the shore. Other causes of pollution included factories along the sound and along rivers that connect to the sound. The pollution killed animals and plants that live in the water. Government leaders and residents of both Connecticut and New York are working to clean up the sound.

The Hills of Connecticut

Away from the Connecticut River and Long Island Sound, hills dot the landscape. The

Hikers enjoy a peaceful trek through the forests in Litchfield Hills as the trees take on the colors of autumn.

area west of the river is called the Western Uplands. In the northwest corner of the state, Connecticut's highest point is the southern side of Mount Frissell, at 2,380 feet (725 m). Mount Frissell is part of a region called the Berkshire Hills. Most of this mountain, including its highest point, is located in Massachusetts. At 2,323 feet (708 m), Bear Mountain is the tallest peak located entirely within Connecticut's borders. It is just east of Mount Frissell. The Appalachian Trail, which stretches from Georgia to Maine, crosses Bear Mountain.

The Western Uplands also have one major river, the Housatonic. This river begins in Massachusetts, runs from the top of the state through the western section, and drains into Long Island Sound. The Housatonic's waters once provided power for many mills and factories. The river's fast-moving water ran generators that created electricity. This kind of electricity is called hydroelectricity or hydropower.

Candlewood Lake takes its name from Candlewood Mountain—so named by early settlers because it is where American Indians showed them how to make candles from pieces of pine log.

Connecticut has more than 150 active dairy farms.

The state's two largest lakes are also in this region. Candlewood Lake and Barkhamsted Reservoir were made not by natural forces, but by people. Candlewood Lake, the state's largest lake, was created in 1928 to provide hydroelectric power. But the lake is also very popular with Connecticut residents and visitors. In the warmer months, the lake fills with boats and swimmers. The lake has 60 miles (97 km) of shoreline and cuts through several towns, where many people have homes along its peaceful shores.

The western town of Kent is home to Kent Falls, a state park that encompasses almost 300 acres (120 hectares). The park features the highest waterfall in Connecticut. It drops around 250 feet (76 m). Visitors hike and picnic along the trails.

The region east of the Connecticut River is called the Eastern Uplands. The Eastern Uplands are not quite as high as the Western Uplands. In some spots, the hills are crammed together. In other places, flat areas of land are good for farming and raising dairy cows. The major river of the region is the Thames. The U.S. government keeps a major naval submarine base at the mouth of the river in New London.

In Their Own Words

Few states have more to offer in natural beauty, in contentment, and in peace.

—a 1938 guidebook to Connecticut

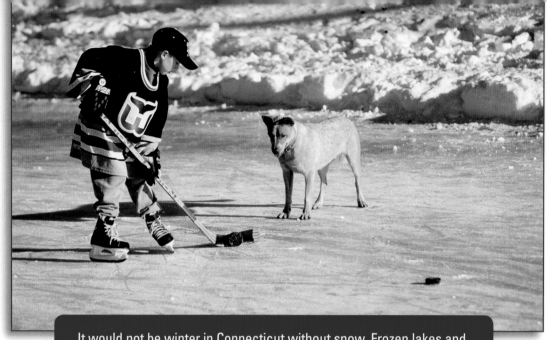

It would not be winter in Connecticut without snow. Frozen lakes and ponds across the state offer many opportunities to enjoy winter sports.

Changing Weather

The weather in Connecticut changes with the seasons. In summer, the air can be humid, and temperatures can go above 90 degrees Fahrenheit (32 degrees Celsius). Autumn tends to be cool and sunny, as the leaves change from green to red, yellow, and gold. In the winter, parts of the state can get more than 4 feet (1.2 m) of snow, but temperatures are usually not bitterly cold. In general, the western hills receive more snow and have colder weather than the rest of the state.

At any time of the year, strong winds and waves from storms can damage houses and flood roads along Long Island Sound. Flooding is common early in the spring. Melting snow along the Connecticut River raises the water level in the state. Connecticut is sometimes hit by nor'easters, large storms that

Quick Facts

DEADLY STORM
Hurricanes do not often reach Connecticut, but when they do, they can be deadly. A hurricane in 1938 remains the state's worst natural disaster. Floods destroyed buildings along Long Island Sound and Connecticut's rivers. The storm was responsible for almost seven hundred deaths across New England.

form when northern and southern storm fronts collide. The amount of snow or rain from a nor'easter can vary from north to south. The Western Uplands might receive as much as 1 foot (30 centimeters) of snow while the shoreline is hit only with rain.

Wildlife of Fields, Forests, and Streams

Connecticut is home to many kinds of trees, flowers, and other plants. Oak, maple, and ash are some of the common leafy trees in the state. The state also has evergreen trees, such as pine and fir. Several types of evergreens are listed as endangered. So are many plants, including the white fringed orchid and the mountain woodfern.

White-tailed deer can be found throughout Connecticut—even in local backyards.

Forests cover around 60 percent of the state. Many different kinds of animals live in these forests and nearby fields. One of the most common mammals is the white-tailed deer. Farmers and homeowners use wire fences or special plantings to help stop deer from eating crops as well as other plants and shrubs. Connecticut also allows deer hunting in certain seasons to prevent the animals from overrunning the state.

The endangered white fringed orchid is native to Connecticut.

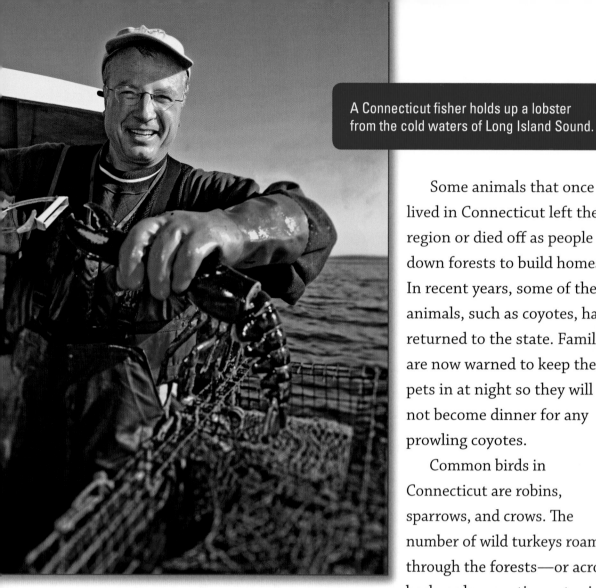

A Connecticut fisher holds up a lobster from the cold waters of Long Island Sound.

Some animals that once lived in Connecticut left the region or died off as people cut down forests to build homes. In recent years, some of these animals, such as coyotes, have returned to the state. Families are now warned to keep their pets in at night so they will not become dinner for any prowling coyotes.

Common birds in Connecticut are robins, sparrows, and crows. The number of wild turkeys roaming through the forests—or across backyards—continues to rise. Bald eagles also live in the state, though they are endangered there. That means there are so few that they might soon disappear from Connecticut entirely.

Many different types of fish swim in Connecticut's waters. Among them is the shad. The roe, or eggs, of this fish are considered a dinner treat. Each May, the town of Windsor has a festival honoring the fish. Salmon were once common in the Connecticut River, but they disappeared. Now the state raises and releases salmon in several of its rivers.

Along Long Island Sound, fishers catch shellfish such as lobsters and oysters. In fact, oysters from Connecticut are the most popular around. People say the cold, salty water contributes to the great taste and texture of Connecticut oysters.

In 1997 and 1998, however, a sudden rise in the water temperature almost destroyed Connecticut's oyster fishing industry. The higher temperature encouraged the growth of small organisms that target oysters. Thousands of acres of shellfish were killed. Today, the oyster beds are once again producing shellfish at a great rate. To prevent this kind of disaster from happening again, scientists are developing a new breed of oyster that grows very fast and is not susceptible to disease.

The use of chemical pesticides, such as DDT, brought the peregrine falcon to the brink of extinction in the United States.

Endangerment

Some animals in Connecticut are considered endangered. This means that their numbers are very small and that they are at risk of disappearing completely. When an animal or plant is listed as endangered, it becomes illegal to kill it or hurt its habitat.

The peregrine falcon is an example of an endangered bird in the state. They are some of the world's fastest birds. When these falcons dive for food, they can reach speeds of 175 miles (282 km) per hour. Peregrines were once common in Connecticut and the rest of North America. By 1950, however, none of these birds were left in the state. They suffered from the use of chemical pesticides and later joined the national list of endangered animals.

The U.S. government worked to increase the number of peregrines. It raised babies and then released them in the wild. In 1997, a pair of peregrine falcons settled in Hartford. They built a nest on the Travelers Tower, one of the state's tallest buildings. The pair then had chicks. The following year, more peregrines returned to Hartford, and several others built nests in nearby cities. Although the peregrine falcon is no longer on the national list of endangered animals, the state of Connecticut still considers it endangered.

Plants & Animals

Black Bear

These bears once filled Connecticut's forests, but their numbers fell as towns grew. By the mid–1800s, they were mostly gone from the state. Black bears started returning to the state after farming decreased and forests began to grow back. Recently, there were almost 1,500 bear sightings in the state.

Black Bass

Two kinds of black bass—smallmouth and largemouth—live in many of Connecticut's lakes and ponds. They eat other fish and insects. Some largemouth bass will even eat birds. Each year, the state adds new bass to lakes, where fishers spend quiet days trying to catch them.

Wild Turkey

Connecticut's first settlers found wild turkeys everywhere. By the early 1800s, however, the bird had disappeared because of hunting and the loss of forests. In recent years, state officials brought wild turkeys back to Connecticut, and now they live in almost every town.

Timber Rattlesnake

One of two venomous snakes in Connecticut, the timber rattler lives in the rocky parts of some forests. Town governments once paid hunters for killing rattlesnakes, but now the reptile is endangered in the state and protected by law.

Maple Tree

Many different kinds of maple trees grow across Connecticut. In the fall, their leaves turn yellow and red, adding to the colors of the season. In March, people tap sugar maples to make maple syrup.

Witch Hazel

In October, this plant blooms with small yellow flowers. Witch hazel is known for the lotion made from its bark and twigs. American Indians showed Connecticut settlers how to use the plant to treat insect bites and wounds. Today, a Connecticut company is one of the world's leading producers of witch hazel.

From the Beginning

The first people to live in Connecticut were various American Indian tribes. They first reached the region about ten thousand years ago. Later tribes included the Pequots, Mohegans, Nipmunks, and Podunks. They spoke a language called Algonquian. As many as ten thousand American Indians may have lived in the area when Europeans first arrived in what became Connecticut.

The Indian tribes raised beans, squash, and corn. They also hunted in the forests and fished in the rivers. The American Indians made their homes from the trees and brush that grew in the woods. They lived off the land, but they also respected it. They hunted only as much as they could eat or use. All parts of the hunted animals were used for things such as food and clothing.

In 1614, a Dutch explorer named Adriaen Block sailed up the Connecticut River almost as far as what is now Massachusetts. He found an Indian fort along the river near the area that became Hartford. More Dutch returned to Connecticut to trade with the American Indians, but they did not settle in the area. The English were the first Europeans to build homes and raise families along the Connecticut River.

First Arrivals

By 1630, two separate groups of English settlers had reached Massachusetts, just north of Connecticut. The Pilgrims lived in Plymouth. In Boston, people known

Boys sell newspapers on the streets of Hartford in 1909.

Puritan religious and colonial leader Thomas Hooker and his followers settled in Hartford in 1636.

as Puritans had just arrived. Both groups were Protestants. They came to North America to practice their religion because England did not give them the freedom to worship as they chose. Besides religious freedom, this new land across the Atlantic Ocean offered settlers a chance to make new and, with luck, prosperous lives.

In 1631, some Podunks from the Connecticut region traveled to Plymouth. They invited the Pilgrims to come live and trade on their land. The Podunks also wanted English military aid to stop raids carried out by the Pequot tribe. In 1633, a small group of English traders built a trading post in what is now Windsor.

That same year, some Puritans explored the Connecticut Valley. One of them said the area had "many very desirable places . . . fit to receive many hundred inhabitants." Soon more English came to trade and then farm along the Connecticut River. The largest group of settlers was made up of Puritans led by Thomas Hooker. He and his group reached Hartford in 1636. Other Puritans went to today's Saybrook, at the mouth of the Connecticut River, and to New Haven, on Long Island Sound.

Although some American Indian groups welcomed the English, others did not. The Europeans brought goods and trade items that proved useful to the Indians. But they also brought diseases to which Indians had no resistance. As a result, many American Indians died of illnesses such as smallpox. Many English settlers also did not respect the Indians' ways of life and their rights to the land. Some English settlers felt that they had a claim to the land even though the American Indians had been living there for years. They did not understand the religions of the Indians and considered them uncivilized people who did not believe in Christianity. Some American Indians were persuaded to become Christians and adopt the ways of the Europeans. Others resisted the English people's growing power.

> # In Their Own Words
>
> *Three and a half centuries ago, the great State of Connecticut began as three small plantations along the Connecticut River. Today, it has grown into what is certainly one of the most progressive and productive states in the United States.*
>
> —former Connecticut governor William O'Neill

The English settlers' relations with the Pequots, in particular, were poor. The Pequots did not want to lose lands to the new arrivals. They stood against the English and the American Indian groups who sided with them. In 1637, small conflicts between the Pequots and the English turned into the Pequot War. The English troops had the support of the Mohegans and their chief, Uncas. They attacked and burned many Pequot villages, killing between four hundred and six hundred tribe members. Some Pequots fled to other villages and eventually adopted the ways of other tribes. Others were captured and sold as slaves to other tribes, to colonial settlers, and to slave traders.

Some historians believe that this defeat of the Pequots was a turning point for English colonization. For the most part, the English did not have to face a

The battles between Pequot Indians and militiamen in 1637 put an end to the Pequot tribe in colonial Connecticut.

large and powerful group of American Indians opposed to their settlements. In addition, the English had other Indian tribes on their side.

Forming a Government and Colony

In 1639, the Hartford settlement drafted rules for forming its own government. Thomas Hooker told the settlers, "The foundation of authority is . . . in the free consent of the people." The settlers would elect others to represent their interests, much as in Massachusetts. However, the Connecticut settlers were the first Americans to write down the rules for their government, called the Fundamental Orders. The rules for forming a government are also called a constitution. Because of the importance of the Fundamental Orders, Connecticut is known as the Constitution State.

Although the English in Connecticut had their own government, they were still tied to England. In 1662, Connecticut received a charter from England.

This legal document made the different settlements in Connecticut part of one colony. The charter also let the residents keep the government they had already formed.

Most English settlers in Connecticut were farmers. They belonged to the Congregational Church, which was the church of the Puritans. Only members of this church could freely practice their religion in the colony. This limit on religious freedom kept other Europeans from coming to Connecticut.

After another Indian war in 1676, known as King Philip's War, Connecticut was mostly peaceful for the English settlers. The Indians, however, were almost wiped out. Many died from illnesses the English brought with them. Others had died in the wars or left the region when they lost their lands.

During the 1700s, the colony began to grow. Farmers raised crops such as corn, rye, and barley. Some residents turned to shipbuilding for work. Others made iron or ground wheat into flour at mills set up along small rivers. Many Connecticut men and women ran various shops, taverns, and inns. In New Haven, students came to one of the colonies' first educational institutions—Yale College, now known as Yale University.

The Fight for Independence

By the mid–1770s, many Americans were calling for independence from England, now a part of Great Britain. In Connecticut, many people supported the call for freedom. Others, however, wanted to remain part of Great Britain. But when the American Revolution began in 1775, Connecticut played an important role. Its early military heroes included Generals Israel Putnam and Benedict Arnold. At

Nathan Hale was born in 1755 in Coventry, Connecticut. He was only twenty-one when the British killed him for spying.

the Battle of Bunker Hill in Boston, Putnam is said to have given the famous order, "Don't fire until you see the whites of their eyes." Arnold is known today as a traitor who tried to surrender the American fort at West Point, New York, to the British. But in the early part of the war, he led American troops in several major battles.

Another Connecticut hero was Nathan Hale, a schoolteacher turned soldier. He served as an American spy at the beginning of the war. Then the British caught and

Quick Facts

CONNECTICUT'S GREATEST LEADER

Jonathan Trumbull was the last colonial governor of Connecticut and the first governor of the state. During the American Revolution, Trumbull was the only colonial governor to side with the colonists. He was therefore the only one to remain in office throughout the war—and to be elected once the colonies gained freedom. Many historians consider Trumbull one of the state's greatest leaders.

hanged him. Before he died, Hale said, "I only regret that I have but one life to lose for my country."

The American Revolution ended in 1783. Connecticut had helped win the revolution in an important way. It provided guns, cannons, and other supplies for the troops. These supplies are also called provisions, and George Washington nicknamed Connecticut the Provisions State. Connecticut's role as a major weapons maker continued to grow after the war. In 1788, five years after the war ended, Connecticut became the fifth state to ratify the new U.S. Constitution.

A Growing State

By the nineteenth century, Connecticut had little farmland left for new settlers. Because of the landscape, it was hard for many farmers to make a living. Connecticut did not provide such abundant crops as states that had much more land that was fertile.

Instead of farming, manufacturing and trade became the center of economic activity. Different cities became famous for different products. Waterbury was the Brass City, and Meriden was the Silver City. Plymouth was a clock-making center. Danbury, called Hat City, was one of the country's leading producers of headwear. In Hartford, banks and insurance companies grew, and the city was known as the Insurance Capital. Shipbuilding also remained important along the Connecticut River and Long Island Sound. The city of New London was the center of Connecticut's whaling trade.

Quick Facts

"I'M A YANKEE DOODLE DANDY"

Connecticut's state song, "Yankee Doodle," gained popularity during the American Revolution. According to legend, a British surgeon named Richard Shuckburgh wrote the lyrics we know today to mock the ragtag appearance of colonial troops. As the colonists began gaining victories over the British, American soldiers adopted the song. Then, as today, Americans sing the song to show they are proud of who they are.

In the nineteenth century, whaling was one of Connecticut's largest industries. Today, visitors at Mystic Seaport can board the *Charles W. Morgan*, a wooden sailing ship once used to hunt whales.

One newspaper writer in the mid–1800s was impressed with the number of talented people who came from the state. "Everybody worth knowing was born in Connecticut—or should have been," the journalist wrote. "It is the most extraordinary patch of land in the known world."

Traders from Connecticut traveled all over the country selling goods made in the state. These people were often called Yankee peddlers. The peddlers sold many items, including nutmeg, a spice from the seed produced by a nutmeg tree. Nutmeg is often used in pies, puddings, cakes, and cookies. Connecticut is often nicknamed the Nutmeg State, and its people are called Nutmeggers.

Connecticut inventors played a large role in building the state's economy. In 1836, Hartford-born Samuel Colt received a patent for a new kind of pistol. The Colt revolver was the first firearm that could discharge five or six times without reloading. Before Colt's invention, only one- or two-barrel flintlock pistols were available. Colt later built a huge factory in Hartford.

The state was also a leader in making machines and tools that made other items. In 1793, a Yale graduate named Eli Whitney had invented the cotton gin (short for *engine*), a machine that separates cotton fibers from the seeds. Whitney then developed the idea for mass production—a faster, less expensive way to manufacture goods. Before this innovation, products such as guns were made one at a time, by hand. It took a lot of time to make each gun, and it was difficult to find replacement parts. Whitney came up with a plan for milling machines that made many identical copies of each gun part. Then workers would assemble the parts quickly and cheaply to make many guns that were exactly the same. Whitney opened a factory in New Haven, and his ideas for mass production spread to other factories throughout the state. Through the nineteenth century, some notable products made in Connecticut included typewriters, bicycles, sewing machines, and textiles for clothing.

The new factories that appeared in Connecticut before and after the Civil War needed workers. Immigrants from Europe began to move to Connecticut in large numbers. The first major wave, from Ireland, took place in the 1840s. Germans also came at this time. In the decades that followed, many people came from southern and eastern Europe. These immigrants included Polish and Italian people. Most newcomers settled in cities to work in factories, but some also bought farms.

Although Whitney's cotton gin brought great wealth to Southern planters, many chose to copy rather than pay for his patented machine. After deciding that "an invention can be so valuable as to be worthless to the inventor," Eli Whitney did not patent his later inventions.

MAKING A PEDDLER'S TRUNK

You can make a peddler's trunk and fill it with a "peddler's load"—the goods they brought from town to town. Before trying this, be sure to get permission to ransack your home for goods to peddle!

WHAT YOU NEED

Large cardboard box with four top flaps

Scissors

Duct tape

Paintbrush

Tempera paint

Large nail

Pen

3 feet (0.9 m) of thin cord or twine

To Make the Peddler's Trunk

Cut the top flaps off the cardboard box. Sometimes cardboard can be tough to cut, so ask an adult for help. Tape the two long flaps together side by side so they can form the lid of the box. Be sure to tape both sides so that the lid will stay in one piece. Paint the outside of the box and lid a dark solid color and let it dry.

Then ask an adult to help you use the nail to poke three evenly spaced holes along the top edge of one long side of the box. The holes should be about 1 inch (2.5 cm) from the top edge of the box. Beside each hole poke another about an inch away. You should have six holes in a row.

Next, make holes along the edge of the lid that match the holes in the box. To do this, have someone hold the edge of the lid behind the holes you poked. Push a pen through one of the holes in the box and draw a small circle on the lid. Repeat with the other five holes. Your circles should be at least an inch from the long edge of the lid. Poke the nail through each circle.

Cut the cord into three pieces, each 1 foot (30 cm) long. Push the end of one piece through a hole from the underside of the lid and out the top. Do the same with the other end of that piece of cord, pushing it through the other hole of that pair on the lid. Now both ends of the cord will be sticking out of the top of the lid. Take those two ends and poke them through the matching pair of holes on the box from the outside in. Leave a little slack. Tie a knot inside the box. Repeat with the other two pairs of holes in the lid and the box, using two more pieces of cord. This will make hinges for the lid of the trunk.

Filling Your Trunk

Fill your trunk with peddlers' goods, such as metal ladles, spoons or combs, scraps of cloth, ribbons, buttons, old eyeglasses, small clocks, and books. Once your trunk is full, peddle the goods around to your classmates, friends, and family, and try to make some deals. Use your most convincing sales pitch and your imagination to describe each item.

Changing Times

While Connecticut was changing, so was the nation. Tensions stemming from differences between the Northern states and Southern states were rising. One reason for the tension had to do with the North's and the South's different economies. Another source of tension was the issue of slavery. The Southern states depended on slavery to keep their agricultural economy going. The Northern states did not have the same need for slaves, and some Northerners believed that slavery was wrong in a free society. These conflicts would lead to the outbreak of the Civil War in 1861.

On July 2, 1839, Joseph Cinqué, a man who had been stolen from his home in West Africa and enslaved, led a revolt on board the *Amistad* slave ship.

...ath of Capt. Ferrer, the Captain of the Ami...

...ose Ruiz and Don Pedro Montez, of the Island of Cuba, having purchased fifty-three slaves at Havan...
...d the Amistad, Capt. Ferrer, in order to transport them to Principe, another port on the Island of Cu...
...s, the African captives on board, in order to obtain their freedom, and return to Africa, armed thems...
...and crew of the vessel. Capt. Ferrer and the cook of the vessel were killed; two of the crew escape...

Like most Northern states, Connecticut had a mixed past when it came to the issue of slavery. Not many slaves lived in the colony in the early 1700s. However, by the start of the American Revolution, Connecticut had the largest number of slaves in New England (though the number of almost 6,500 was nowhere near numbers in the South). Free blacks in Connecticut also suffered from discrimination, and runaway slaves were always prosecuted and returned to their masters. The Connecticut legislature rejected bills to free enslaved blacks three times—in 1777, 1779, and 1780.

On the other side of the issue were groups in the state who worked tirelessly to end slavery. They were able to get a gradual emancipation act passed in 1784. Slavery was finally abolished in the state in 1848. Even while slavery was still legal in Connecticut, some people worked to help escaped slaves when they could.

From the 1830s until the end of the Civil War, the Underground Railroad helped slaves from the South find freedom in free states. The railroad was a network that consisted of white abolitionists (people who believed slavery was wrong and fought against it), free blacks, and escaped slaves. Conductors—the people who would lead the escaped slaves north to freedom—met the slaves at a designated point in the South and led them north at night. Others gave the conductors and slaves shelter and food. Sometimes the slaves traveled all night or hid in tunnels or hidden passageways. Researchers have identified many buildings in Connecticut as stops along the Underground Railroad. These sites are honored as part of the Connecticut Freedom Trail.

The story of the *Amistad* is another example of how Connecticut played a part in the fight against slavery. In 1839, a group of African slaves revolted against their captors on the ship *Amistad*. The vessel

d, July, 1839.

ntly imported from Africa, put them fter being out from Havana about ith cane knives, and rose upon the iz and Montez were made prisoners.

eventually arrived in New London, and the Africans spent more than a year in jail in New Haven, hoping to win their freedom in court. With the legal help of former U.S. president John Quincy Adams, the Africans were allowed to go home. Before leaving the United States, they spent almost a year in Farmington, where the local people housed, clothed, and educated them. Connecticutians also helped raise money for the Africans' journey back home. The incident has been called the most important battle for civil rights in Connecticut.

The Civil War was fought from 1861 to 1865. Connecticut sent more than 50,000 men to fight for the Union (the United States) against the Confederacy (the eleven Southern states that had seceded from, or left, the United States). Included was an African-American military unit called the Connecticut Twenty-Ninth Colored Regiment. Connecticut also supported the war effort by providing weapons, clothing, and food to the Union soldiers.

After the Civil War

After the Confederacy was defeated and the Civil War ended, life in the state changed. By 1910, almost all Nutmeggers lived in cities and towns instead of on farms. Farmland was better in the Midwest and West, so those areas of the country took over growing the crops to feed the nation. As a result, industry was the major source of jobs in Connecticut. Many Nutmeggers started to work in factories. During World War I, which lasted from 1914 to 1918, the state supplied guns and other weapons. After the United States entered the war in 1917, Connecticut once again provided the nation with brave men and women who served in or worked for the military.

World War II, which took place from 1939 to 1945, brought even more changes. Supplying engines and other parts for airplanes became the state's major industry even before the United States entered the fight in 1941. Across Connecticut, women went to work in the factories to provide supplies and equipment during the war.

Another change was the growing African-American population. Black people had lived in Connecticut since colonial times. The first Africans were brought to

During World War II, women filled many jobs formerly held by men. This woman worked at Groton's Electric Boat Company, which manufactured submarines and patrol torpedo, or PT, boats.

the state at a time when slavery was legal. A smaller number settled in Connecticut as free people. During World War II, northern factories needed workers, and many African Americans from the South headed to Connecticut for jobs.

Into the Modern Era

Since World War II, many manufacturing companies and other businesses have moved out of the state. More people now work in the service industry. This includes banks, government agencies, schools and other educational institutions, and companies that provide services to tourists. New industries and businesses continue to create jobs. The insurance companies in the state still employ many Nutmeggers. Connecticut is also becoming a major center for scientific and medical research. Stamford, in particular, has seen an increase in media companies. World Wrestling Entertainment (WWE), Arts and Entertainment (A&E) Networks, and the Yankees Entertainment and Sports (YES) Network all have offices or their headquarters in the city.

Connecticut also continues to attract people from other countries. Along with their cultures, many of these immigrants bring new ideas to the state. The ideas that come from the state's residents help Connecticut continue to grow and move into the future.

Quick Facts

A FAMILY OF POLITICIANS
Though often connected with Texas, the Bush family has strong roots in the Nutmeg State. George H. W. Bush was born in Milton, Massachusetts, in 1924 and moved to Greenwich with his family the same year. His father, Prescott, served as a U.S. senator from Connecticut from 1952 to 1963. Like his father, George graduated from Yale University. He also entered politics and, in 1988, was elected president, defeating Massachusetts governor Michael Dukakis. Son George W. (also a graduate of Yale) was elected president in 2000.

Important Dates

★ **1614** Dutch explorer Adriaen Block sails up the Connecticut River.

★ **1633** The Dutch build a fort in what is now Hartford. English settlers from Massachusetts begin exploring Connecticut.

★ **1637** The English settlers defeat the Pequots in the Pequot War.

★ **1639** Voters in Hartford accept the Fundamental Orders, which outline how the government will run.

★ **1662** Connecticut receives a charter from the English government.

★ **1775–1783** The American Revolution is fought.

★ **1764** The *Connecticut Courant* publishes its first issue. Now called the *Hartford Courant*, it is the nation's oldest newspaper in continuous publication.

★ **1788** Connecticut becomes the fifth state to ratify the U.S. Constitution.

★ **1828** Noah Webster publishes the first important dictionary of American English.

★ **1848** Slavery is abolished in Connecticut.

★ **1855** Samuel Colt opens his new firearms factory in Hartford.

★ **1861–1865** The Civil War is fought.

★ **1917** The U.S. Navy opens a submarine school in Groton.

★ **1938** A hurricane, which kills almost seven hundred people, becomes the state's worst natural disaster.

★ **1954** The *Nautilus*, the world's first nuclear-powered submarine, launches from Groton.

★ **1974** Ella Grasso becomes the first woman governor of Connecticut.

★ **1988** Nutmegger George H. W. Bush is elected president.

★ **2000** Democratic senator Joe Lieberman of Stamford becomes the first Jewish vice-presidential candidate from a major party.

★ **2004** The UConn men's and women's basketball teams win the NCAA championship, making UConn the first school to win both Division I titles in the same year.

The People

The original inhabitants of the land that is now called Connecticut were the American Indians. They lived there for thousands of years before Europeans ventured across the ocean. From the late 1600s until the 1820s, most people who lived in Connecticut came from England or other parts of Great Britain. Almost all of them were Protestants. The state had a small, steady population.

Since the 1800s, Connecticut has become more diverse, with citizens coming from many different countries. Every ten years, the U.S. government counts the number of people living in the United States. This count is called the census. Between censuses, the U.S. Census Bureau estimates the size of each state's population. According to the 2007 Census Bureau estimate, Connecticut had a little more than 3.5 million people.

The number of non-Hispanic white people in the state has fallen in recent years. Meanwhile, Hispanic, African-American, and Asian-American populations have risen. Hispanics now make up more than

Quick Facts

STEADY AS SHE GOES
Connecticut earned one of its nicknames, Land of Steady Habits, from the fact that the Puritans who lived in the state behaved according to a strict code about what is right and wrong.

Like the beautiful flowers that thrive in Connecticut's many gardens and parks, diversity blooms in the state.

People of many religions live side by side in Connecticut. Here, men pray at the United Muslim Masjid in Waterbury.

11 percent of the state's residents. A majority are of Puerto Rican descent, but many Connecticut Hispanics are from elsewhere in Latin America. African Americans comprise approximately 9 percent of the state population. Asians make up about 3 percent of the population.

The people of Connecticut practice many different religions. The largest group is Roman Catholic. Many others belong to various Protestant churches. These include Congregational, Episcopal, Lutheran, Methodist, and Baptist. Jewish settlers first came to Connecticut in the 1700s, and recently, Russian Jewish immigrants have come to the state. Many newer immigrants from Eastern Europe and Asia practice religions such as Islam, Buddhism, and Hinduism. The people from these different cultures and religions have helped to shape Connecticut into the culturally diverse state it is today.

In Their Own Words

Connecticut from the mid-nineteenth century on has been a very urban, very ethnic, . . . varied kind of place, even though it's small.

—historian Herb Janick

Return of the Natives

In 1980, only about 4,000 people in Connecticut considered themselves American Indians. In the 2007 census estimate, about 35,000 people said they were part or completely American Indian. Most of this growth came after the Mashantucket Pequot and Mohegan tribal nations received federal recognition from the U.S. government. The recognition means that the tribes can run their lands as separate nations.

Many members of these tribes—and others—had left Connecticut in the past and have since returned to their tribal lands. One Pequot who returned was Denise Porter. She said, "I felt that [the tribal nation] was part of me. . . . I thought, 'This is good because I'm back home and I'm working for my own people.'" Connecticut's returning American Indians are able to share their heritage while living on their tribal lands. And with federal recognition, they can also run businesses of their choice. The Pequots and Mohegans have used

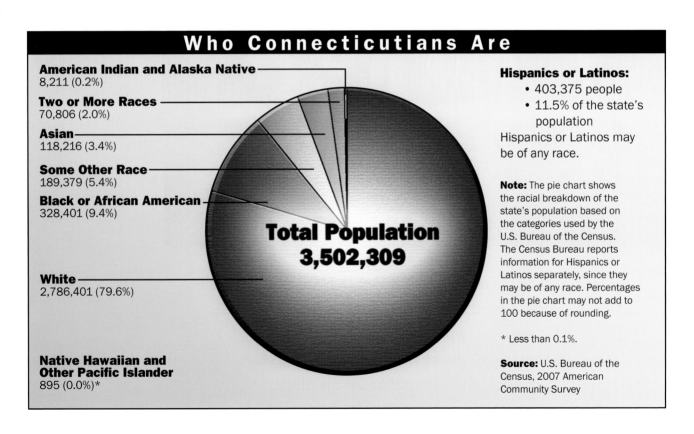

Who Connecticutians Are

American Indian and Alaska Native
8,211 (0.2%)

Two or More Races
70,806 (2.0%)

Asian
118,216 (3.4%)

Some Other Race
189,379 (5.4%)

Black or African American
328,401 (9.4%)

White
2,786,401 (79.6%)

Native Hawaiian and Other Pacific Islander
895 (0.0%)*

Total Population
3,502,309

Hispanics or Latinos:
- 403,375 people
- 11.5% of the state's population

Hispanics or Latinos may be of any race.

Note: The pie chart shows the racial breakdown of the state's population based on the categories used by the U.S. Bureau of the Census. The Census Bureau reports information for Hispanics or Latinos separately, since they may be of any race. Percentages in the pie chart may not add to 100 because of rounding.

* Less than 0.1%.

Source: U.S. Bureau of the Census, 2007 American Community Survey

Events such as this Mashantucket Pequot Tribal Nation powwow held in North Stonington give American Indians a chance to celebrate—and share—their traditional lifeways.

the land to build casinos, which have earned hundreds of millions of dollars. The money goes toward maintaining their lands and businesses and funding education for their young people.

The Mashantucket Pequots are also interested in sharing their history and culture with others. They have established the Mashantucket Pequot Museum and Research Center. It includes full-size exhibits of Pequot farmers and hunters that show details of life from the past and present. Visitors are welcome to read more about Pequot history in Connecticut at the center's archives.

Some American Indian groups stayed in Connecticut even after they lost their traditional lands. The Schaghticoke Reservation is located on the New York–Connecticut border in Litchfield County. The Paucatuck Eastern Pequot Reservation is in New Windsor. These groups are proud of their heritage and often travel to schools and events across Connecticut to teach others. After a long battle, the Schaghticoke people gained federal recognition in 2004. Other groups, such as the Eastern Pequots, are still seeking recognition from the U.S. government.

Every year about 250,000 people visit the tribally owned and operated Mashantucket Pequot Museum and Research Center to learn about the Indians and natural history.

Famous Nutmeggers

Noah Webster: Teacher and Writer

Noah Webster was born in West Hartford in 1758. He worked as a schoolteacher, and in 1783, he wrote a book to teach students grammar. Webster noticed that Americans spelled some words differently from the British (*color* instead of *colour*, for example). Americans also used words not used in England. In 1828, he published the first dictionary of American English.

Prudence Crandall: Teacher and Crusader

Prudence Crandall was born in Rhode Island in 1803. In 1831, she opened a school for girls in Canterbury, Connecticut. About two years later, an African-American girl was accepted as a student—a first for New England. Outraged whites demanded that the girl be expelled. Instead, Crandall opened a school for black children. After withstanding violent protests, much harassment, and a stint in jail, Crandall was forced to close the school. She died in 1890. Crandall today is remembered as the official state heroine of Connecticut.

Harriet Beecher Stowe: Writer and Abolitionist

Stowe was born in Litchfield in 1811. She wrote more than thirty books before her death in 1896, including *Uncle Tom's Cabin*, a book about the evils of slavery. The best-selling book, which led more people in the North to oppose slavery, has never been out of print. According to legend, when President Abraham Lincoln met Stowe in 1862 during the Civil War, he said, "So you're the little woman who wrote the book that started this Great War!"

Mark Twain: Writer

Twain was born in Missouri in 1835. His real name was Samuel Clemens. He was already a well-known author when he settled in Hartford in 1871. Twain built a huge home that the local newspaper called "one of the oddest-looking buildings in the state ever designed for a dwelling." Twain called it a combination of a river steamboat and a cuckoo clock. In this house, he wrote some of his most famous books. Twain also lived briefly in Redding, where he died in 1910.

Jim Calhoun: UConn's Winningest Coach

Although he was born in Massachusetts in 1942 and grew up there, Calhoun is one of Connecticut's most famous residents. Calhoun came to the state in 1986, charged with the task of turning around the poorly performing UConn men's basketball team. Not only did the Hall of Fame coach meet that challenge, he transformed the program into one of the nation's best.

Glenn Close: Actress

Glenn Close was born on March 19, 1947, in Greenwich. She began acting at a young age and formed her own theatrical group in high school. After college, Close spent six years on the stage before landing her first role in a feature film, *The World According to Garp*. Younger fans probably identify Close with her portrayal of Cruella De Vil in the live-action movie *101 Dalmatians*. In addition to her award-winning film work, Close continues to perform on stage and on TV.

Connecticut is constantly building toward a brighter future.

People on the Move

Most Connecticut residents live in cities or suburbs. The populations of these cities and towns have changed in recent years. The state's largest cities are Bridgeport, New Haven, Hartford, and Stamford. Except for Stamford, all these cities lost population during the 1990s. Some of these cities' residents moved to other towns or smaller cities in the state. They might have moved to find better or different jobs or to raise their families in the quieter suburbs.

Hartford had the largest drop in population, as more than 18,000 people moved out. In 2001, in an effort to bring new life to the capital city, Hartford broke ground on a building project called Adriaen's Landing. Today, the site includes a convention center, a four-star hotel, and a state-of-the-art science center. In 2006, construction began on Front Street, an area that will include shopping, entertainment, and residences.

Hartford and Connecticut's other cities have large African-American and Hispanic populations, but more of these people are moving into towns just outside the cities. Today, a large number of people from different races and backgrounds are spread throughout the state.

Rich State, Poor State

As Connecticut's population changes, the state faces a growing problem. Many people have good jobs and live well, particularly in some of the suburbs of Fairfield and Hartford counties. For example, in Fairfield County's New Canaan and Darien, the average annual family income is more than $200,000. This area near Long Island Sound is sometimes called the Gold Coast. Some of the wealthiest towns in the United States can be found there. But not all the towns and cities in Fairfield and Hartford counties are as prosperous. Many towns are populated mostly with middle-class families. Still, because of the Gold Coast, people often assume that all of Connecticut is wealthy.

The truth, however, is that the state has a large gap between its rich and poor. In the cities and in some rural parts of the state, people have trouble finding jobs. In Hartford County, almost 10 percent of residents live below the poverty line. The income level there has fallen in recent years. Poor families in other cities and towns have also seen their income drop.

This gulf between rich and poor is obvious in some of Connecticut's schools. The state boasts several of the nation's top private schools, including Choate, Cheshire Academy, and Hotchkiss. Many of the state's cities and towns also have highly regarded public school systems in which students, on average, do very well academically. However, some of Connecticut's public schools are at the other end of the spectrum.

This difference was brought to the public's attention in 1996 when Milo Sheff, a student at a Hartford middle school, sued the state. He claimed he was being denied equal education. He and the other students who sued with him argued that minority children in cities such as Hartford do not get the same education as the schoolchildren in the state's suburbs and smaller towns. Sheff and the

Connecticut's lawmakers work to make sure children get a quality public education. These students learn at a New Haven middle school.

others wanted the state to provide equal education for all students, regardless of where they lived. The case, known as *Sheff v. O'Neill*, went all the way to Connecticut's supreme court. The court ruled that the state had an obligation to make sure that all Connecticut children have access to equal levels and standards of education.

Connecticut also has many highly regarded colleges and universities. In addition to its prestigious private institutions,

Quick Facts

FIRST IN THE LAND
The first law school in America, Litchfield Law School, was founded in Connecticut in 1784. Famous graduates include former U.S. vice president Aaron Burr, educator Horace Mann, and dictionary author Noah Webster.

Connecticut has a well-respected state university system, which includes the University of Connecticut. These public institutions offer students excellent higher education at an often more affordable price.

The Best of Connecticut

Connecticut offers many reasons for people to live in the state. Some residents like the state's location. It is close to two major cities, New York and Boston, but it also has plenty of woodlands and open spaces. For people who enjoy boating, Long Island Sound is nearby. Some of New England's best mountains for skiing are also next to the state.

Connecticut's largest businesses provide good jobs. Connecticut has highly educated workers skilled in such areas as computers, engineering, and insurance.

The University of Connecticut, founded in 1881, has six campuses and almost 30,000 students.

The Peabody Museum of Natural History at Yale University is a great place to learn about the natural and cultural world.

Face painting is one of many fun offerings at New Haven's annual Festival of Arts and Ideas.

The state's hospitals do important medical research. Overall, Connecticut's public schools are among the best in the nation.

Its cities offer plenty of art and entertainment. Hartford's Wadsworth Atheneum, one of the oldest public art museums in the United States, owns more than 45,000 pieces of art from around the world. Bridgeport is home to the state's only zoo, the Beardsley. Its New World Tropics Building features animals from the rain forests of South America.

In New Haven, Yale University's Peabody Museum displays some of the first dinosaur bones found in North America. Each June, the city sponsors the Festival of Arts and Ideas. Performers entertain on city streets and in theaters across New Haven. The state also has amusement parks, shopping malls, and other places that are perfect for relaxing and having fun. Connecticut has a lot to offer residents and visitors.

Calendar of Events

★ **Three Kings' Day Parade in Hartford**

January 6 is Three Kings' Day, part of the Christmas celebration. To celebrate, Hartford's Hispanic community holds a parade and gives gifts to children.

★ **Open Cockpit Sundays in Windsor Locks**

On several Sundays throughout the year, the New England Air Museum lets visitors explore the cockpits of some of the aircraft on display.

★ **Shakespeare on the Sound**

Every summer, this theater troupe produces free outdoor festivals in Connecticut, with performances in Rowayton and Greenwich.

★ **Boom Box Parade in Willimantic**

When DJs at a local radio station heard there was no band to play in Willimantic's Fourth of July parade, they decided to provide the tunes. In what has become an annual tradition, this parade consists of marchers—anyone is welcome to join in—who carry radios tuned to the same station.

★ **Barnum Festival in Bridgeport**

Every July, all month long, Bridgeport honors its most famous resident, circus owner P. T. Barnum. The festival has circus performances, music, parades, and fireworks.

★ **Hartford Festival of Jazz**

For one weekend in July, Hartford's Bushnell Park is filled with the sound of music, as top jazz artists perform free concerts.

★ Italian Festival in Enfield

Many Connecticut towns host festivals celebrating the state's Italian immigrants. The Enfield festival, usually held in August, is one of the oldest. The fun includes games, music, rides, and of course, plenty of Italian food.

★ International Festival of Puppet Arts in Storrs

In September, the University of Connecticut brings in puppeteers from around the world for this festival for both children and adults.

★ Oyster Festival in Norwalk

Each year in September, Norwalk celebrates its most famous shellfish with food, music, and harbor cruises.

★ Apple Fest in Glastonbury

October is harvesttime, and this festival pays tribute to Connecticut's farming roots. The festival features a pie bake-off and a pie-eating contest, as well as rides, crafts, food, and entertainment.

How the Government Works

Since colonial days, residents of Connecticut have taken a strong interest in their government. The Fundamental Orders of 1639 said that the people had the right to choose their leaders. They also had the right to limit the power of those leaders.

England chose the governors for most of its colonies. But in Connecticut, the people elected their governor. In towns, people came out every year for town meetings. Voters decided how a town should spend its money and run its affairs. Today, Connecticut has 169 towns, and each likes to be as independent as possible. Local control and the power of each person's vote are still important in Connecticut.

Local Government

Connecticut towns and cities can decide how they run their local governments. This is called home rule. In each Connecticut town, voters elect a number of people to carry out town affairs. These elected officials are called representatives. They go by different names, depending on the town's type of government.

Some small towns call each of their representatives a selectman. He or she often serves on a board of selectmen. Towns that have selectmen usually have town meetings throughout the year to debate and vote on important issues that affect residents.

The Connecticut State Capitol, opened in Hartford in 1878, became a Registered National Historic Landmark in 1971.

Branches of Government

EXECUTIVE ★ ★ ★ ★ ★ ★ ★ ★

This branch includes the governor, lieutenant governor, secretary of state, treasurer, and attorney general. The governor either approves or vetoes (rejects) laws passed by the legislature. Then the governor and other executive agencies make sure these laws are carried out. The governor also proposes and works with the state budget that determines how much money the state will spend and what it will be spent on. He or she also appoints other state officials. Governors are elected for four-year terms.

LEGISLATIVE ★ ★ ★ ★ ★ ★ ★ ★

The state house of representatives and state senate form the General Assembly, Connecticut's legislative branch. Legislators propose and pass laws for the state. The senate has 36 members and the house of representatives has 151 members. All are elected for two-year terms.

JUDICIAL ★ ★ ★ ★ ★ ★ ★ ★

The court system decides whether people accused of crimes have actually broken a law. The courts also rule on disputes between individuals or companies. In addition, the courts can decide if state laws are legal under the Connecticut constitution. The judicial system includes superior courts for most criminal trials and lawsuits brought by one citizen against another. Court decisions can be appealed to appellate courts and then to the state's highest court, the supreme court of Connecticut.

Larger towns and cities call their representatives council members. They form a town or city council. Sometimes these towns also have a manager. This person is hired by the council to help run the town.

In some cities, voters elect a mayor. A mayor's power can vary. Depending on the city, the mayor can run the town as a council or board of selectmen would, or he or she serves as a contact between the community and the local city government.

Counties are groups of towns and cities located near one another. Connecticut has eight counties: Hartford, New Haven, Fairfield, Middlesex, Litchfield, Windham, Tolland, and New London. Unlike most states, Connecticut does not have county governments. This is sometimes a problem for government planning. Because towns and cities work so independently, they often do not work together to create and support legislation that goes beyond their home-rule area.

Higher Levels of Government

Connecticut's state government is similar to the U.S. government. It has three parts, or branches. The three branches exist so that one branch does not have too much power. They keep each other in check.

As of 2010, Connecticut had seven members of the U.S. Congress in Washington, D.C. Five served in the U.S. House of Representatives, and two served in the U.S. Senate. Voters in each of five regions, called districts, elected one House member. Voters from across the state elected the U.S. senators.

Members of the Connecticut General Assembly are sworn in as part of opening day ceremonies at the Connecticut State Capitol in Hartford on January 7, 2009.

How a Bill Becomes a Law

When the state faces challenging issues, state legislators often propose laws (called bills until they are passed) to address them. Sometimes the ideas behind a bill come from the state's residents. The senator or representative who came up with the idea must introduce the bill in his or her house. A committee of representatives or senators (depending upon where the bill starts) discusses and perhaps alters the bill. If the committee approves the bill, it goes to all the members of the house in which it originated. If they vote to approve it, the bill moves to the other house. Members in that house then discuss the bill. If they vote to approve the bill, it goes to the governor. If they approve a revised version of the bill, the revised bill may go back to the first house for approval. In some cases, members from both houses get together to make the two versions of a bill passed by both houses into one final bill. Then both houses must vote to approve it.

When a bill passed by both houses gets to the governor, he or she can accept or reject the bill. When the governor accepts it, it becomes a law. When he or she rejects a bill, that action is called a veto. Sometimes a bill can become law if the governor takes no action and neither accepts nor rejects it. If the governor vetoes the bill, it can still become a law if two-thirds of the members in each house vote to override the veto.

The Courts in Action

The judicial system also has a powerful role in how the state's laws are interpreted and enforced. For example, in 2001, Connecticut's judges played a large role in changing how residents use the state's beaches. A 1919 law gave the town of Greenwich the right to allow only town residents to use its public beach along Long Island Sound. Other towns along the shore also limited the use of their beaches. A Stamford lawyer named Brendan Leydon thought it was unfair for the towns to limit his right to use the public beaches. In 1994, he sued the town of Greenwich. He claimed he had a legal right to use the beaches.

For seven years, the case went through the Connecticut courts. Leydon's case seemed to threaten the history of local control, which is very important to

Connecticut towns. It also touched on the growing gap between the state's rich and poor people. Greenwich and many other towns along the shore are wealthy. By closing the beaches to residents from other towns, some people thought Greenwich wanted to keep poor people out of the town. But others felt that

In 2010, the Connecticut Supreme Court in Hartford celebrated its 200th anniversary.

the tax-paying residents of Greenwich had special rights to the beach.

A lower state court ruled against Leydon. Another court said he was right. Finally, the case reached the state supreme court. It ruled that Leydon and other Connecticut residents had a legal right to use the beaches.

Despite the ruling, two of Greenwich's beaches remained effectively closed to nonresidents for several more years. Island Beach and Great Captain's Island can be reached only by private boat or ferry. Until 2007, the ferries were off limits to nonresidents. Greenwich selectman Peter Crumbine realized that it was probably just a matter of time before the town faced another lawsuit. In 2007, he overturned the policy and made ferry rides available to out-of-towners.

A Greener Way

Some lawmakers and citizens have also taken steps to make Connecticut a greener state. In September 2008, Westport's legislative body passed a bill banning the use of plastic shopping bags. Under the rule, a store that distributes plastic bags can be fined $150. The ban went into effect on March 19, 2009.

Although many citizens and environmental groups applauded the measure, some grocery chains were opposed. A little more than half a year into the program, legislative member Jeffrey Weiser calculated that residents had used two fewer plastic bags per week per household. That adds up to at least 600,000 fewer plastic bags. Some in Westport say the bag ban has increased awareness of other green alternatives, such as organic farming.

Greenwich Point Park, also known as Tod's Point, is a local favorite that is now open to nonresidents.

Making a Living

Connecticut's workers have jobs that are both old and new. Farmers still raise crops and animals, just as the American Indians and first settlers did. Factory workers turn out equipment and weapons for the military, as early Connecticut craftspeople did. But the state is also part of cutting-edge industries, with computers and other high-tech tools, and Connecticut workers look to the future with biotechnology, using science to create new drugs, plants, and even animals. Many of Connecticut's businesses are also part of the media and entertainment industries.

From the Earth

Connecticut farmers produce more than $600 million worth of agricultural products each year. Food products include fruits, vegetables, and dairy products. Connecticut also has many nurseries. These special farms raise plants and trees that are used to decorate lawns and other outdoor spots. Plants grown in the state are also sold and shipped to other states.

Although Connecticut is a small state, it leads New England in growing pears and peaches. Connecticut farms also grow apples, different types of berries, tomatoes, corn, and other vegetables. The state's farmers are among the country's top producers of mushrooms. Connecticut dairy farmers get more milk from each of their cows than do farmers in other states in the region.

Home to many corporate headquarters and countless small businesses, Stamford is known as "the city that works."

Another crop is shade tobacco, which grows along the Connecticut River. Farmers raise tobacco in covered fields and then dry it in special barns. Most of the crop is used to wrap high-quality cigars. As of 2007, tobacco was the number one agricultural export in Connecticut, contributing about $63 million in income to the state.

Sometimes it costs too much to run a farm. An easier way for farmers to make money is to sell their farms to corporations that would like to develop—or build on—their land. Connecticut loses some farmland each year to development. A state program called the Farmland Preservation Program gives farmers money so they can keep working their land instead of selling it to developers who build houses, stores, or offices.

Connecticut also has a large aquaculture industry. This is the raising of fish and other water animals for food. Many Connecticut companies raise oysters. In the United States, only Louisiana produces more oysters.

Rocks and minerals also come from the earth. Unlike many states, Connecticut does not have a large mining industry. Most of what is mined is sand and small stones used in construction.

In the summer, Connecticutians can pick their own peaches at orchards like this one.

RECIPE FOR APPLE CRISP

Connecticut's juicy Cortland apples draw apple pickers from all around. This dessert is a treat on a chilly fall or winter day. It is delicious fresh out of the oven with a scoop of vanilla ice cream.

WHAT YOU NEED

Filling:

4 cups (about 1 liter) sliced and peeled Cortland apples

$1/2$ cup (100 grams) granulated sugar

$1/2$ teaspoon (2.5 g) cinnamon

Topping:

1 cup (220 g) brown sugar

$1^1/_4$ cups (160 g) all-purpose flour

1 cup (85 g) rolled oats

$1/2$ teaspoon (2.5 g) salt

$1/2$ cup (113 g) butter

$1/3$ cup (76 g) shortening

Have an adult help you preheat the oven to 375 °F (190 °C). Mix the apple slices, granulated sugar, and cinnamon in a large bowl. Transfer to a greased 8-by-8-inch (20-by-20-cm) baking pan. To make the topping, sift the flour into a clean bowl. Add the brown sugar, oats, and salt. Using a pastry cutter or a fork, mash in the butter and shortening. Sprinkle the topping mixture over the apples in the pan. Bake for 40 minutes until the topping is crisp and brown. Ask an adult to help you remove the crisp from the oven and serve it.

Manufacturing

Connecticut has lost many manufacturing jobs in recent years. Some companies moved out of state. Others that used to work for the U.S. military received fewer orders to make goods, so the companies had to lay off workers. However, manufacturers in Connecticut still make many things. About one out of every eight workers is in manufacturing.

The state's largest manufacturing companies build aircraft engines, helicopters, and submarines. Other companies make metal parts that are used in aircraft engines and other large pieces of equipment. Some companies also make the machines that make these parts. Producing all these things requires skilled workers. Connecticut is known for its well-trained machinists and engineers.

Connecticut is also the home to many interesting—and fun—products. Connecticut is the birthplace of the Wiffle ball. The plastic bats and balls are still made in the state. Another Connecticut product is PEZ. Since 1972, all the PEZ eaten in the United States has come from a factory in Orange, Connecticut.

Connecticut companies make parts for aircraft, such as this jet engine.

Workers & Industries

Industry	Number of People Working in That Industry	Percentage of All Workers Who Are Working in That Industry
Education and health care	407,789	23.4%
Wholesale and retail businesses	251,220	14.4%
Manufacturing	214,847	12.3%
Professionals, scientists, and managers	183,858	10.6%
Publishing, media, entertainment, hotels, and restaurants	180,995	10.4%
Banking and finance, insurance, and real estate	169,751	9.7%
Construction	119,148	6.8%
Other services	75,566	4.3%
Transportation and public utilities	67,110	3.9%
Government	65,145	3.7%
Farming, fishing, forestry, and mining	6,853	0.4%
Totals	1,742,282	100%

Notes: Figures above do not include people in the armed forces. "Professionals" includes people such as doctors and lawyers. Percentages may not add to 100 because of rounding.

Source: U.S. Bureau of the Census, 2007 estimates

Quick Facts

THE NAME GAME

The first PEZ, a compressed peppermint candy, were made in Vienna, Austria. The name comes from the German word for peppermint—*PfeffErminZ*. They are now produced in south-central Connecticut and come in many flavors.

This is good for the state's economy since Americans eat more than 3 billion PEZ each year!

Making Modern Technology

Connecticut's long history as a place for new technologies and inventions continues today. The state is a leader in the field of biotechnology. Scientists are studying genes, which are tiny chemicals found in every living thing. Genes control how a plant or animal looks and how it survives. Scientists can use different genes to create new drugs, treat some illnesses, or make plants that grow faster. Connecticut is becoming a center for biotechnology research.

Connecticut companies of all sizes also use science and computers to create other things. Small computer software businesses have been coming to the state. Other state companies are involved with the Internet and making computer parts.

One teenage Connecticut inventor turned to science to create a new product. In 2001, Michael Nyberg of Old Lyme found that certain high sounds can kill mosquitoes before they become adults. The adult mosquitoes bite people and sometimes carry deadly diseases, such as West Nile virus. "I knew I wanted to do a project in acoustics [sound]," Nyberg said. "We had this big West Nile scare, and I . . . kind of put the two together." For a science project, Nyberg built a device, now called the Larvasonic, to test his idea about using sound to kill the mosquitoes. Now he and his family run a company to sell the machines.

The Travelers Tower (far left) is one of downtown Hartford's landmark buildings.

A Good FIRE and Growing Service

About 170,000 Nutmeggers work in a group of industries sometimes called FIRE: finance, insurance, and real estate. In Connecticut, the largest of these are insurance and finance. The state's first insurance company opened in Hartford in 1810. Today, Stamford is a financial center because it is so close to New York City. Many financial companies based in New York have offices in the area. Some companies have even moved their headquarters from New York City to Stamford.

The Mohegan Sun Resort and Casino draws visitors from around the world.

Companies involved in FIRE are sometimes called service industries. Other service jobs include selling goods in stores, providing legal services and medical care, and working for schools. More than 800,000 Nutmeggers work in these other service industries. Another 65,000 work for the government at the local, state, and national levels.

Tourism

Tourism is one part of the service industry that has grown in Connecticut. People from around the country—and around the world—like to visit Connecticut for several reasons. In the fall, many visitors come to parts of the state to admire the beautiful scenery and the colorful foliage. People visit the state during other parts of the year, looking to relax in the peace and quiet of Connecticut's countryside. They might also want to visit historic spots, such as the Mystic Seaport restored whaling village and Connecticut Freedom Trail sites honoring the state's African-American heritage.

The state's cities also have a lot to offer tourists, including museums and fine restaurants. Many Nutmeggers work in the theaters, museums, and stores that tourists often visit. Whatever their reasons, and whichever part of the state tourists visit, they will need to stay and eat at Connecticut's hotels and restaurants. Not only do these businesses bring money into the state, but they also provide jobs for many Nutmeggers.

A large part of the state's growth in tourism can be credited to the two casinos and resorts operated by American Indian tribes. Foxwoods, owned by the Mashantucket Pequot tribal nation, is the largest casino in the world. Mohegan Sun is run by the Mohegans. In 2001, the tribe opened several new buildings, and its casino is now the second largest. The two casinos, as well as the hotels, restaurants, and other facilities that are part of the resorts, provide many jobs in the southeastern part of the state. Singers and other entertainers often perform at the resorts. Their shows draw residents and tourists alike. The casinos also pay millions of dollars in taxes to the state each year. Other state tribes hope to build casinos in the future.

Products & Resources

Aerospace Technology

Aerospace technology includes the manufacturing of aircraft and other equipment used in air and space travel. Connecticut is a leading producer of aerospace products. Many of the helicopters and aircraft engines designed and made in Connecticut are used by the U.S. military.

Submarines

Connecticut has a long history of making the world's best submarines. The U.S. Navy relies on Connecticut workers to build fast and silent subs.

Medical Research

In laboratories across the state, Connecticut scientists look for medicines that can cure or prevent sickness. The state's universities also contribute to the medical research needed to help people.

Fruits

Connecticut farmers grow fruits such as pears, peaches, and apples.
Many Connecticut-grown products are shipped to other states.
They are also sold at local farmers' markets and at roadside stands.

Tourism

Tourism is a major source of jobs in Connecticut, where people come to experience beautiful fall foliage, live entertainment, and marine life. At the Mystic Aquarium and Institute for Exploration, visitors can feel the splash of a beluga whale and touch a cownose ray.

Seafood

The seafood industry is very important to Connecticut. Millions of pounds of seafood are harvested every year, bringing more than $100 million to the state's economy. Oysters, shrimp, and shad are just some examples of Connecticut seafood. The state's seafood festivals and restaurants also bring in money.

Mystic Seaport's living-history museum is just one of Connecticut's investments in the future.

What Does the Future Hold?

The economy across the United States began to suffer in 2008. As the country entered a severe recession, many people lost their jobs. Workers in Connecticut felt the effects of the weak economy. But Connecticut still produces many items important for the country's defense. As the U.S. government continues to spend money for high-tech equipment for the military, Connecticut companies should benefit.

Among all U.S. states, Connecticut has one of the highest percentages of residents who are college graduates. These educated workers will continue to make useful new products and start new companies. Yankee ingenuity is still strong in Connecticut. Nutmeggers from all walks of life and all different fields will work together to help their state continue to grow and move into the future.

State Flag & Seal

Connecticut's flag shows the state coat of arms on a blue background. The streamer below the shield has the state motto in Latin. Qui Transtulit Sustinet *means "He Who Transplanted Still Sustains."*

The state seal bears the same symbols as the coat of arms. It is believed that the three grapevines represent early colonial settlements in the area. The Latin translation for "Seal of the State of Connecticut" is printed around the seal. This version of the seal was adopted in 1931.

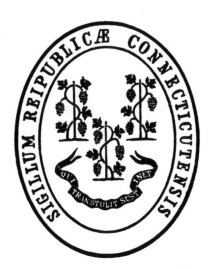

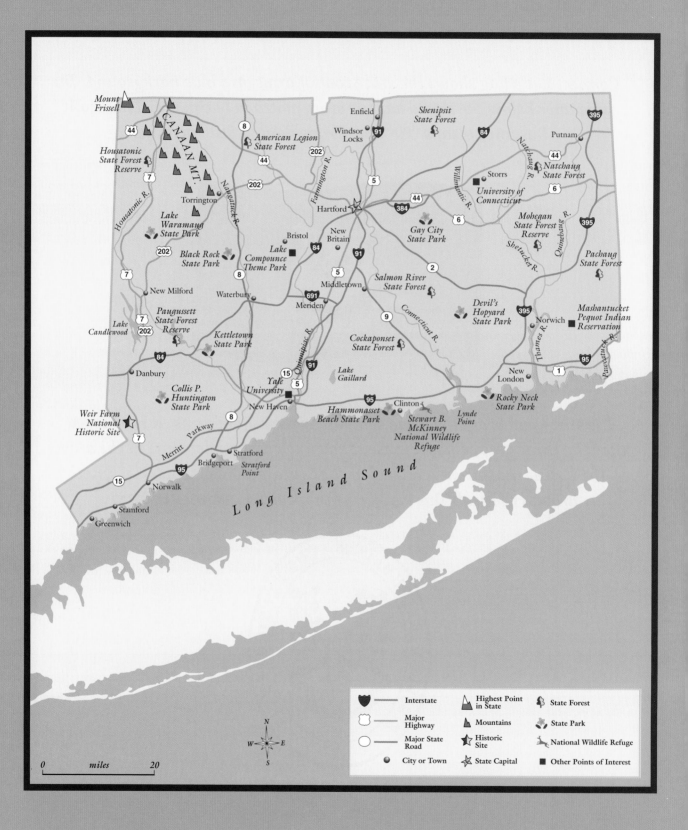

Mount
Frissell

CANAAN MT.

44

Housatonic
State Forest
Reserve

7

Housatonic R.

Naugatuck R.

Torrington

Lake
Waramaug
State Park

202

8

American Legion
State Forest

44

202

Enfield

Windsor
Locks

91

202

Shenipsit
State Forest

84

Natchaug R.

Putnam

395

44

Storrs

6

Natchaug
State Forest

University of
Connecticut

Willimantic R.

Hartford

384

44

6

Mohegan
State Forest
Reserve

Shetucket R.

Quinebaug R.

395

Pachaug
State Forest

Black Rock
State Park

Lake
Compounce
Theme Park

Bristol

New
Britain

84

91

Gay City
State Park

2

Salmon River
State Forest

5

New Milford

8

5

Middletown

Devil's
Hopyard
State Park

Mashantucket
Pequot Indian
Reservation

395

Waterbury

691

Meriden

9

Cockaponset
State Forest

Connecticut R.

Norwich

Thames R.

95

1

Lake
Candlewood

7

202

Paugussett
State Forest
Reserve

Kettletown
State Park

Quinnipiac R.

91

Lake
Gaillard

New
London

Pawcatuck R.

84

Danbury

Collis P.
Huntington
State Park

15

5

Yale
University

Rocky Neck
State Park

Weir Farm
National
Historic Site

7

8

New Haven

Merritt

Parkway

Stratford

95

Bridgeport

15

Norwalk

Stamford

Greenwich

Hammonasset
Beach State Park

95

Clinton

Lynde
Point

Stewart B.
McKinney
National Wildlife
Refuge

Stratford
Point

Long Island Sound

N
W   E
S

0   miles   20

	Interstate		Highest Point in State		State Forest
	Major Highway		Mountains		State Park
	Major State Road		Historic Site		National Wildlife Refuge
	City or Town		State Capital		Other Points of Interest

State Song

Yankee Doodle

words and music by unknown

Yan - kee Doo - dle went to town, Rid - ing on a po - ny,

Stuck a fea - ther in his hat, And called it ma - ca - ro - ni.

Chorus

Yan - kee Doo - dle keep it up, Yan - kee Doo - dle dan - dy,

Mind the mus - ic and the step, And with the folks be hand - y.

BOOKS

Alexander, Elizabeth, and Marilyn Nelson. *Miss Crandall's School for Young Ladies & Little Misses of Color*. Honesdale, PA: Wordsong, 2007.

Azarian, Melissa Eisen. *The Amistad Mutiny: From the Court Case to the Movie*. Berkeley Heights, NJ: Enslow Publishers, 2009.

Burgan, Michael. *Voices from Colonial America: Connecticut 1614–1776*. Washington, DC: National Geographic Children's Books, 2007.

Gibson, Karen Bush. *Eli Whitney*. Hockessin, DE: Mitchell Lane Publishers, 2006.

Haugen, Brenda. *Harriet Beecher Stowe: Author and Advocate*. Mankato, MN: Compass Point Books, 2006.

Lefkowitz, Arthur. *Bushnell's Submarine*. New York: Scholastic, 2006.

WEBSITES

ConneCTkids—The Official State of Connecticut Website for Children:
http://www.kids.ct.gov/kids/site

Mashantucket Pequot Museum and Research Center:
http://www.pequotmuseum.org

Mystic Seaport:
http://www.mysticseaport.org

Michael Burgan, born and raised in Connecticut, graduated from the University of Connecticut with a degree in history. He has written more than 150 fiction and nonfiction books for children, as well as articles for adults. He has written several books on U.S. history, World War II, the Cold War, and U.S. foreign policy. Burgan is a recipient of an Educational Press Association of America award.

Stephanie Fitzgerald has been writing nonfiction for children for more than ten years, and she is the author of more than twenty books. Her specialties include history, wildlife, and popular culture. She lives in Stamford, Connecticut, with her husband and their daughter.

INDEX

Page numbers in **boldface** are illustrations.